INSIDE
EARTHQUAKES

by Melissa Stewart

Illustrations throughout by Cynthia Shaw

STERLING CHILDREN'S BOOKS
New York

STERLING CHILDREN'S BOOKS
New York

An Imprint of Sterling Publishing
387 Park Avenue South
New York, NY 10016

© 2011 by Melissa Stewart

Designed by Anke Stohlmann Design.

ISBN 978-1-4027-5877-5 (hardcover)
ISBN 978-1-4027-8163-6 (flexibound)

Distributed in Canada by Sterling Publishing
c/o Canadian Manda Group, 165 Dufferin Street
Toronto, Ontario, Canada M6K 3H6
Distributed in the United Kingdom by GMC Distribution Services
Castle Place, 166 High Street, Lewes, East Sussex, England BN7 1XU
Distributed in Australia by Capricorn Link (Australia) Pty. Ltd.
P.O. Box 704, Windsor, NSW 2756, Australia

For information about custom editions, special sales, and premium and corporate purchases, please contact Sterling Special Sales at 800-805-5489 or specialsales@sterlingpublishing.com.

Printed in China
Lot #:
10 9 8 7 6 5 4 3 2 1
07/11

www.sterlingpublishing.com/kids

IMAGE CREDITS:

Alamy: © mediacolor's: 24 (2); © Japan Stock Photography: 24 (4)

AP Photo: © Bill Roth/Anchorage Daily News/AP Photo: cover; © David Guttenfelder/AP Photo: 4&9; © Chiaki Tsukumo: 17; © Binsar Bakkara: 21; © Nancy Taggart/The Richmond Register: 28 bottom; 35 bottom; © Ian McKain: 38; © Ted S. Warren: 39

Corbis: © Will & Deni McIntyre: 7; © Craig Aurness: 11 bottom; © Joseph Sohm: 14 (1); © Roger Ressmeyer: title page; 14 (2), 24 (5); © Luis Enrique Ascui: 15; © David Gray/Reuters: 19; © Gary Fiegehen/All Canada Photos: 20 top; © Lloyd Cluff: 20 bottom; © Mark Downey/Lucid Images: 22; © Dai Kurokawa/epa: 24 (3); © Michael S. Yamashita: 24 (6), back cover; © epa: 24 (7); © Reuters: 28 top; © MJ Kim/Hope for Haiti Now/PictureGroup: 28 middle; © HO/Reuters: 29; © Bettmann: 31, 34; 35 top; © Reuters: 36; © Blaine Harrington III: 44 top

Getty: © Jim Wark/Visuals Unlimited: 10; © L. Toshio Kishiyama/Flickr: 11 top; © Digital Globe: 18 top & bottom; © James A. Sugar/National Geographic: 45

Image Works: © TopFoto: 14 (4)

iStockphoto: © NickMattiuzzo: 40

Landov: © Kyodo: 42

Library of Congress: 14 (5)

NASA: 12

PAKSBAB: 44 bottom

Photo Researchers, Inc: © Tom McHugh: 24 (1); © Byron Jorjorian: 37

Superstock: © SSPL: 41

USGS: 2–3, 30, 14 (3)

ON SHAKY GROUND

Imagine lying in your bed. Just as you're drifting off to sleep, the bed suddenly shakes—just a little bit. A couple of books fall off a shelf. What's going on? It's a minor earthquake.

More than one million earthquakes, or temblors, shake our planet every year, but we don't even notice most of them. About ten thousand of those earthquakes do some minor damage, but only two or three cause major destruction.

What causes earthquakes? Forces at work deep inside our planet cause the ground to rumble and shake. The earth below our feet may seem steady and stable, but it's not. Earth's rocky surface and the materials inside are always on the move.

On March 11, 2011, the ground shook violently in northern Japan as one of the five most powerful earthquakes ever recorded struck just 45 miles (72 kilometers) off the coast. The quake triggered a tsunami that thrust waves up to 97 feet (30 meters) tall onto shore just a few minutes later. This photo shows the devastation in the city of Minamisanriku. Ninety-five percent of the city's buildings were destroyed and half the people living there died.

A CRACK IN THE EARTH

Layers of Earth

Earth's uppermost layer, or crust, is broken into slabs of rock called tectonic plates. These plates float on top of the mantle, a thicker layer that contains hot, soft rock called magma. Like cooked oatmeal, magma is thick, but it can flow.

The heat that keeps magma partially melted comes from Earth's fiery center. As heat escapes from the inner and outer cores, it pushes magma upward. Meanwhile, cooler magma at the top of the mantle moves down to take its place.

Over millions of years, magma slowly circles through the mantle—and the tectonic plates go along for the ride. On average, Earth's plates move about 2 inches (5 centimeters) each year. Your fingernails grow at about the same rate.

The thin, outer layer of our planet is called the crust. The next layer, the mantle, contains magma that is always on the move. The core consists of an outer liquid layer and a solid inner layer.

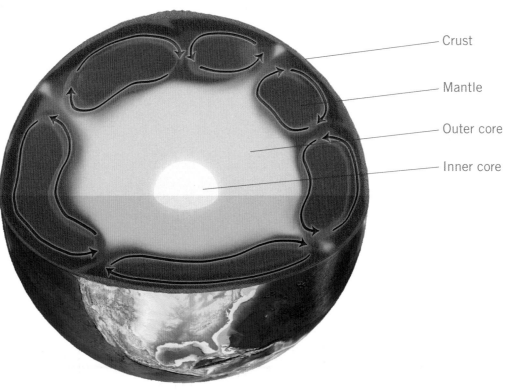

Crust

Mantle

Outer core

Inner core

Waves of Destruction

As tectonic plates move, Earth's rocky crust is pushed and pulled, scraped and jostled. Stress and strain slowly build. Eventually, the crust reaches its breaking point. It suddenly cracks and shifts, releasing waves of energy called an earthquake. The waves radiate in every direction, and the ground shakes up and down and from side to side.

The point where earthquake waves begin—the place where rocks crack and shift—is called the focus. The area on Earth's surface directly above the focus is called the epicenter. During an earthquake, the strongest shaking occurs at the epicenter. As the waves spread, they become weaker.

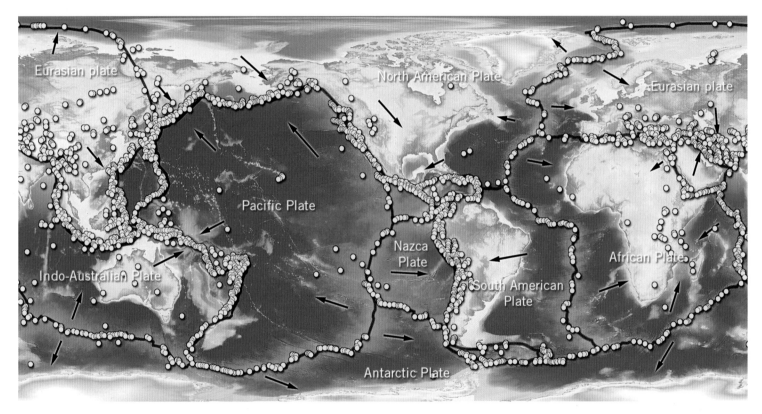

As you can see from the pattern of yellow dots on this map, most earthquakes occur along the edges of tectonic plates.

Ancient Earthquakes

Long ago, people thought that water or the tension between water and earth caused earthquakes. Pliny the Elder, a Roman naturalist and philosopher who lived about 2,000 years ago, called earthquakes "underground thunderstorms."

CONTENTS

How to read this book

This book is different from most books you read. Many of its pages fold out—or flip up! To know where to read next, follow arrows like these (↑), and look for page numbers to help you find your place. Happy exploring!

Quake Patterns

An earthquake can occur any time, any place, but most happen along the edges of tectonic plates. That's where rocks in the crust are under the most stress.

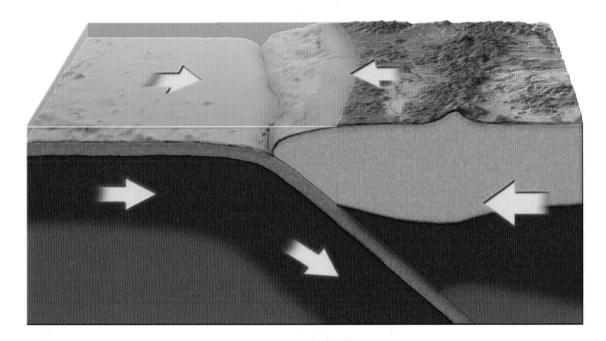

Crash and Slide

About 90 percent of all earthquakes occur along the edges of the Pacific Ocean, where thin ocean plates crash into—and then slide below—thicker continental plates. As a thin tectonic plate is pushed down into the mantle, the thicker plate crumples and buckles. Both motions cause pressure that can lead to earthquakes.

Bump It Up!

Earthquakes also strike in a zone that extends from the Mediterranean region through Turkey and Iran to northern India and China. Throughout this area, mountains are rising as continental plates collide and one tectonic plate is forced below the other.

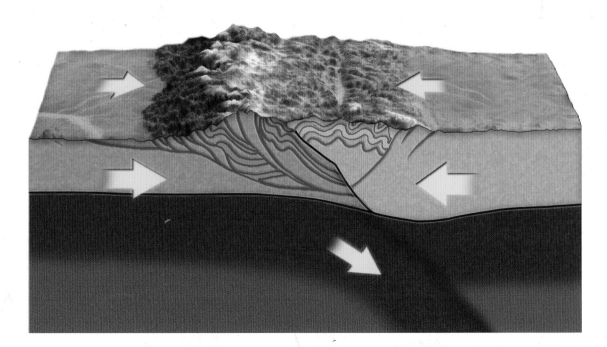

A California quake tore apart the ground underlying this road.

WHAT'S AT FAULT?

Three Kinds of Faults

Most earthquakes occur along faults—breaks that form at or below the surface as rocks shift underground. Most faults occur in places where two or more plates meet. Not all faults behave in the same way, so scientists divide them into three categories.

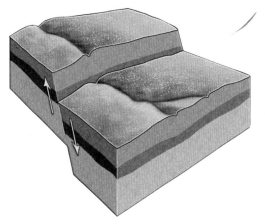

Normal Fault

When rocks pull away from one another, the land on one side of the break slips downward. As a result, the land on the other side of the break becomes noticeably higher. As the land continues to move apart, a series of parallel normal faults may form. This aerial view shows that process currently happening in the Basin and Range region of the western United States.

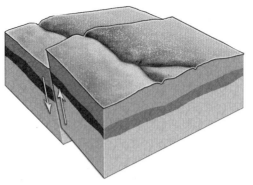

Thrust Fault

When rocks are pushed together, the rock on one side of the break rides up over the rock on the other side. A thrust fault usually occurs in places where plates are colliding. Thrust fault activity formed Virginia's Humpback Mountain, shown here, and the rest of the Appalachian Mountains Range in the eastern United States.

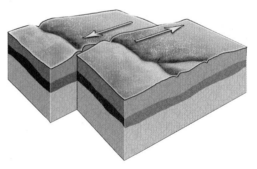

Lateral Fault

When the land on either side of a break moves in opposite directions or at different speeds, a long, wide crack is visible on the ground, but the land on either side does not move up or down. The San Andreas Fault in California, shown here, is one of the longest lateral faults in the world.

Epicenter:
Angeles
National
Forest, east
of Santa
Clarita

in property damage.

4

**Kern County
Earthquake**

July 21,
1952

Epicenter:
23 miles
south of
Bakersfield

When the White Wolf Fault
slipped, people reported vibrations
as far away as Reno, Nevada.
The earthquake claimed 12 lives
and caused at least $48 million
in property damage.

5

**Great San
Francisco
Earthquake**

April 18,
1906

Epicenter:
Off the
coast of San
Francisco

When a 296-mile (476-km)
section of the San Andreas
Fault suddenly shifted, people
felt the shaking from Oregon
to Los Angeles. At least two
thousand people died in
San Francisco. Most of the
buildings that didn't collapse
were destroyed by fires that
raged for three days.

I Was There!

Two weeks after the 1906 quake, survivor Warren Olney wrote the following descriptions in a letter to a friend.
"Did you ever see a dog shake a rat? We were like rats in a dog's mouth. Old Mother Earth appeared to be trying
to shake us off her face. . . . I have been over a great battlefield before the dead were buried and of course it
was a most gruesome sight, but a dead city with its blackened and charred ruins is almost as dreadful."

California Quakes

California experienced five major earthquakes during the twentieth century. Each one devastated towns and cities close to the epicenter.

1

Northridge Earthquake

January 17, 1994

Epicenter: Los Angeles

When rocks in the Oak Ridge Fault Zone suddenly slipped, the shaking quake completely destroyed or damaged bridges, ramps, roadways, and interchanges on four freeways. It devastated apartment buildings, parking structures, and office buildings throughout Los Angeles. Many homes in the San Fernando Valley and Santa Monica areas collapsed. The quake killed 72 people.

2

Loma Prieta Earthquake

October 17, 1989

Epicenter: Nisene Marks State Park, 10 miles northeast of Santa Cruz

At least 63 people died when a break along the San Andreas Fault shook San Francisco, Oakland, Santa Cruz, and the Monterey Bay for 15 seconds. The temblor caused about $6 billion in property damage and interrupted the World Series.

3

San Fernando Earthquake

February 9, 1971

As the San Fernando Fault ripped a 12-mile (19-km) long gash across Earth's surface, buildings and freeway overpasses collapsed. The temblor killed 65 people and caused more than $500 million

The San Andreas Fault

The San Andreas Fault is a 660-mile (1,062-kilometer)–long zone of weakness that runs along the California coast. It is the longest, most active break in a network of faults that slice the state in two. San Diego and Los Angeles are located on the west side of the fault, and Sacramento and San Jose are on the east side. The fault runs directly beneath San Francisco.

The San Andreas Fault formed about 15 million years ago, when the Pacific Plate and the North American Plate began moving in opposite directions. Today the Pacific Plate slowly slides northwest, while the North American gradually grinds its way southwest.

Not all of the land along the San Andreas Fault moves at the same rate. In some areas, the land creeps a few inches each year. In other areas, the land remains still for decades or even centuries.

In places where the rock on either side of the fault is locked together, stress slowly increases over time. Finally, the rock snaps, causing a major quake. Scientists predict that Californians have a 65 percent chance of experiencing another major quake before 2040.

Fault Line

Have you ever wondered what the San Andreas Fault would look like from 45,000 feet (13,725 meters) above Earth? This dramatic three-dimensional view shows the part of the fault near San Francisco, California. The image was captured by radar equipment onboard a research aircraft.

Believe It or Not

Some scientists say that earthquake activity will eventually cause the western part of California to break away from the eastern half. They predict that western California will become a long, thin island that slowly moves away from the mainland.

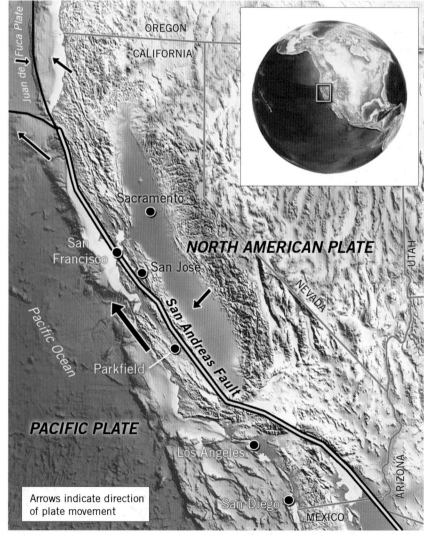

Arrows indicate direction of plate movement

As the North American Plate pulls away from the Pacific Plate, the state of California is slowly being torn apart. People living along the San Andreas Fault can expect more quake activity in the future.

Tsunami

Before the Tsunami

As you can see in this aerial photo, before the 2004 Indian Ocean earthquake shook the seafloor near Sumatra, Indonesia, for nearly 10 minutes, the city of Banda Aceh was one of Indonesia's most important port cities.

After the Tsunami

Banda Aceh was the closest major city to the 2004 Indian Ocean earthquake's epicenter. It was devastated by the earthquake. Then about 15 minutes later, the city was flooded and many buildings were washed out to sea by a tsunami—a towering wall of water formed as shifting rocks within the crust caused the ocean to slosh back and forth. This photo shows the damage.

FROM BAD TO WORSE

More Troubling Tremors

When Earth's crust suddenly cracks and shifts, the rock all around it must adjust. Over the next few days, weeks, months or even years, the rock close to the earthquake's focus may move or crack too, causing more vibrations. The earthquakes that follow a large quake are called aftershocks. Aftershocks are weaker than the original quake, but they can still cause death and destruction.

A man and child ride past buildings reduced to rubble by a massive aftershock of the 2004 Indian Ocean earthquake. The temblor devastated Gunungsitoli, the largest city on the Indonesian island of Nias, and killed 1,300 people and destroyed hundreds of buildings.

The Danger Continues

During a major earthquake, buildings collapse and roads are destroyed. Cell-phone towers topple to the ground, making it hard for people to communicate. Power lines snap and power-generating facilities may be damaged, cutting off electricity to nearby towns and cities. If nuclear power plants are affected, dangerous radioactive materials may escape into the air. People fear for their lives and worry about family and friends.

Everyone feels relieved when the shaking stops. But that may not be the end of the trouble. Earthquakes can cause fires and floods. They can also trigger tsunamis, landslides, and avalanches.

Fire

The earthquake that struck Kobe, Japan, in January 17, 1995, broke pipes carrying natural gas and snapped power lines all over the city. More than three hundred fires, like the one shown in this photo, broke out when leaking natural gas came into contact with live electrical wiring. Because debris blocked many roads, it took firefighters two days to put out all the fires. The fires killed 500 people and destroyed nearly 7,000 buildings.

SIZING UP EARTHQUAKES

Two Kinds of Scales

Scientists currently use two different kinds of scales to measure the size and strength of temblors. The measurements allow them to compare earthquakes that occur in different parts of the world.

In the early 1900s, Italian scientist Giuseppe Mercalli became one of the earliest scientists to create a scale based on an earthquake's intensity. It reports how people experience an earthquake and how much damage it causes. A modified version of Mercalli's scale is still in use today.

In 1935, an American scientist named Charles Richter developed a scale that reports an earthquake's magnitude—the amount of energy it releases. Scientists used the Richter's Scale for many years. But in 1979, American scientist Thomas Hanks and Japanese scientist Hiroo Kanamori introduced an even more powerful scale for measuring an earthquake's magnitude. This newer scale, the Moment Magnitude Scale, is what most scientists use today.

While earthquakes with magnitudes as low as 5 or 6 can cause some damage, it takes a moment magnitude score of 7 or greater for an earthquake to be considered "major." A major quake causes enough destruction to seriously interfere with people's lives.

Lift the flap on the next page to learn more about how the intensity and magnitude of earthquakes are related.

After the Loma Prieta earthquake shook the California cities of San Francisco, Oakland, Santa Cruz, and the Monterey Bay in 1989, scientists assigned it a score of 6.9 on the Moment Magnitude Scale. That makes it one of the ten most powerful temblors to rock California during the twentieth century.

The 2004 Indian Ocean tsunami radiated out in every direction. Within a few hours, huge waves had reached Sri Lanka, Thailand, and southern India. The tsunami affected areas more than 5,000 miles (8,000 km) away from the site of the earthquake. About 16 hours after the quake, a 5-foot (1.5-m) tall wall of water crashed onto the shores of Struisbaai, South Africa. Wherever it struck, the tsunami destroyed everything in its path. More than 228,000 people living in 15 countries died during the tsunami, and another 1.7 million people lost their homes.

Flood

On May 12, 2008, an earthquake rocked the Sichuan Providence in central China and reduced dozens of towns and villages to rubble. More than 68,000 people died and at least 4.8 million were left homeless. Over the next few weeks, more than thirty "quake lakes" formed as massive amounts of water built up behind earthquake debris blocking local rivers. On June 10, 2008, water broke through the debris damming one of the rivers and flooded Beichuan, China, the city shown in this photo.

Landslide

On January 9, 1965, an earthquake near Hope, British Columbia, triggered one of the largest landslides ever recorded in Canada. As the 2-mile (3.2-km) wide mass of pulverized rocks and mud slid down the 6,000-foot (1,830-m) mountainside shown in this photo, it buried four people and their cars under 300 feet (92 m) of material. Then it filled in a lake, plowed up the other side of the valley, and finally flowed back up the original slope.

Avalanche

On July 9, 1958, an earthquake triggered a massive avalanche on a slope above Lituya Bay, Alaska. When the mass of ice and rock hit the water, it created the tallest wave ever documented. As you can see in this photo, the powerful wave stripped all the trees off this rocky ridge and washed them into the bay.

On September 29, 2009, earthquake activity devastated Padang, West Sumatra's capital city, and surrounding areas. As you can see in this photo, many roads were damaged by the shaking. In addition, nearly 280,000 homes were damaged or destroyed and at least 1,100 people died.

Shake, Rattle, and Roll

The 2004 Indian Ocean earthquake was so powerful that scientists in Oklahoma could detect its vibrations. The quake released about the same amount of energy as 100 gigatons of dynamite. If all that energy could have been harnessed, it could have powered all the homes and businesses in the United States for six months.

In December 2004, the third most powerful earthquake ever recorded shook Sumatra, Indonesia, and other nearby islands in the Indian Ocean. People felt some mild aftershocks over the next few weeks, but one tremendous aftershock in March 2005 took everyone by surprise. It turned out to be the seventh largest earthquake on Earth since 1900.

Another major tremor shook the area in September 2007, but scientists still didn't think the danger had passed. At the time, John McCloskey, a researcher at the University of Ulster in Ireland, called Sumatra "the most likely place on the planet" for another large quake.

And McCloskey was right. Another major temblor struck in September 2009. Scientists worry that even more earthquakes will shake the region as the Indo-Australian Plate continues to slide under the Eurasian Plate.

5.0–5.9	VI–VII	VI. Felt by all. People have trouble walking. Some heavy furniture moves. Dishes break and pictures fall off walls. VII. People have trouble standing. Furniture breaks; plaster and bricks may crack and fall. Noticeable waves form on ponds. Church bells ring.	
6.0–6.9	VIII–IX	VIII. People have trouble driving cars. Walls, chimneys, and tree branches break and fall. Some buildings may collapse. IX. People panic. Underground pipes may break, and many buildings are damaged. The ground may crack.	
7.0–7.9	X–XI	X. Many buildings collapse. Water splashes over the banks of rivers and canals. Railroad tracks bend. XI. Highways, railroad tracks, bridges, and underground pipelines are destroyed. Most buildings collapse. Large cracks appear in the ground.	
8.0 or greater	XII	XII. Complete destruction of buildings and transportation. The surface of the ground moves in ripples or waves. The ground is covered with cracks and holes.	

QUAKES TO REMEMBER

2010 Haiti Earthquake

Where: Port-au-Prince, Haiti
When: January 12, 2010
Magnitude: 7.0

As the Caribbean Plate grinds past the North American plate, pressure slowly builds within the surrounding rock. At 4:53 p.m. on January 12, 2010, the rocky crust about 8 miles (13 km) below Haiti finally reached its breaking point. It suddenly slipped nearly 6 feet (1.8 m), sending out powerful waves of energy in every direction.

Within minutes, more than 280,000 buildings in Port-au-Prince, Haiti's capital city, were reduced to rubble. The quake killed 220,000 people and injured 300,000 others. It was the biggest temblor to hit the region in 240 years and the fifth deadliest in recorded history.

The earthquake caused more than $1 billion in damage and left at least as 1.4 million people homeless. Experts say it will take the tiny Caribbean country many years to recover from the devastation.

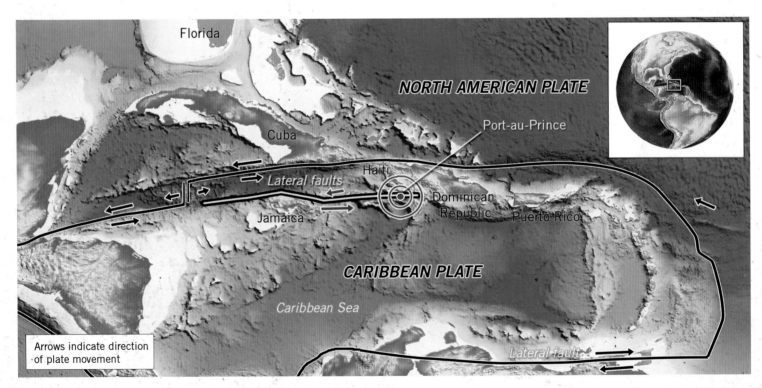

Florida

NORTH AMERICAN PLATE

Cuba

Port-au-Prince

Lateral faults

Haiti

Dominican Republic

Puerto Rico

Jamaica

CARIBBEAN PLATE

Caribbean Sea

Lateral fault

Arrows indicate direction of plate movement

Before the 2010 Haiti Earthquake, the Enriquillo-Plaintain Garden Fault—a lateral fault that runs directly below southern Haiti—had been locked in place for 250 years. As the Caribbean Plate moved past the North American Plate, stress built up inside the crust. Finally, the rock fractured, creating a 40-mile (65-km)-long crack in the crust.

Biggest Isn't Always Baddest

The 2004 Indian Ocean earthquake was one of the most powerful tremors ever recorded, so it's no surprise that it killed so many people. But the largest earthquakes don't always do the most damage. In fact, most of the deadliest temblors in history had magnitudes between 7 and 8.

The July 1976 earthquake in Tangshan, China, had a magnitude of 7.5. Why was it the third deadliest quake of all time? Because it shook an area where lots of people lived. Many of the world's largest cities are located near faults. As the human population continues to grow, smaller earthquakes are likely to cause even more death and destruction.

The Ten Deadliest Earthquakes in Recorded History

Location	Number of People Killed	Magnitude	Date
Shaanxi, China	830,000	8.0	1556
Sumatra, Indonesia	283,000	9.1	2004
Tangshan, China	255,000	7.5	1976
Aleppo, Syria	230,000	Unknown	1138
Port-au-Prince, Haiti	220,000	7.0	2010
Damghan, Iran	200,000	Unknown	856
Haiyuan, Ningxia, China	200,000	7.8	1920
Ardabil, Iran	150,000	Unknown	893
Kanto, Japan	143,000	7.9	1923
Ashgabat, Turkmenistan	110,000	7.3	1948

Comparing the Moment Magnitude and Modified Mercalli Scales

Magnitude Scale (Moment Magnitude)	Intensity Scale (Modified Mercalli)	Effects Felt by People Nearby
1.0-3.0	I	I. Shaking is rarely felt by people.
3.0-3.9	II–III	II. Only people at rest feel the shaking, especially if they are on the upper floors of a building. Suspended objects may swing. III. Many people indoors feel shaking, but most people do not recognize it as an earthquake.
4.0–4.9	IV–V	IV. Most people indoors and some outdoors notice shaking. Dishes, windows, and doors rattle. Walls creak. Parked cars rock. V. Felt by almost everyone. Many sleeping people wake up. Liquid splashes out of glasses. Small objects are knocked over. Some dishes and windows break.

The January 14, 2010 earthquake devastated all the homes along this hillside in Port-Au-Prince, Haiti.

I Was There!

In January 2010, Kim Bentrott was working as a missionary in Port-au-Prince, Haiti. She wrote a blog post about the earthquake on January 14. "[W]e heard a groaning. Then the building started to tremble. . . . My first thought was that our landlord's truck was rumbling or exploding under the balcony, then that our building was collapsing. . . . We all clung to each other and huddled under a door jam as our apartment pitched, shook, and moaned. We watched the neighbor's balcony seemingly rise up toward us. . . . When the shaking stopped, all fell quiet in the house, but screams were heard on the street."

The World Comes Together

When a major earthquake occurs, people all around the world spring into action. Within 24 hours of Haiti's deadly disaster, rescue workers, peacekeeping troops, and supplies began arriving from other countries.

Help from Foreign Governments

Haiti's next-door neighbor, the Dominican Republic, sent food, water, and machinery to help rescue people. Iceland, Qatar, and Israel provided mobile kitchens and hospitals as well as doctors, nurses, and cooks. After just four days, more than 250 tons of relief supplies had reached Port-au-Prince. The United States, Canada, and countries throughout Europe promised Haiti more than $1 billion in aid.

Earthquake survivors unload food donated by the United Nations World Food Program. Helicopters carrying the food landed in Léogâne, Haiti, a port town located 18 miles (29 km) from Port-au-Prince.

Great Alaskan Earthquake

Where: Prince William Sound, United States
When: March 27, 1964
Magnitude: 9.2

Say the word *earthquake* and most people in North America think of California, but the Golden State isn't the site of the continent's most powerful temblor. On March 27, 1964, a quake with a magnitude of 9.2 shook southern Alaska for four minutes. The earthquake occurred as 30 feet (9 m) of the Pacific Plate was suddenly thrust under the North American Plate.

While many homes and businesses were destroyed in Alaska's major cities, only fifteen people died when buildings collapsed. But that's not the end of the story. The quake triggered an open-ocean tsunami. It also caused an underwater landslide that sent a 230-feet (70-m) tall local wave crashing onto the shore. In the end, more than one hundred people were killed in Alaska, California, and Oregon.

Thousands of aftershocks followed the quake. At least twenty of them had magnitudes of 6.0 or greater. It took more than a year for the crust below Prince William Sound to stabilize.

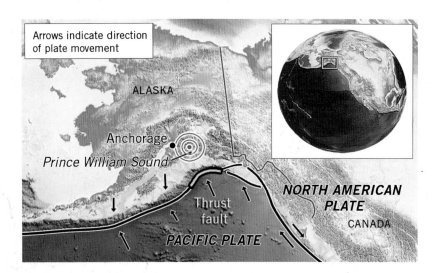

Arrows indicate direction of plate movement

ALASKA

Anchorage
Prince William Sound

Thrust fault

NORTH AMERICAN PLATE
CANADA

PACIFIC PLATE

What caused the Great Alaska Earthquake? The ground surrounding Prince William Sound suddenly shifted because the crust along the Alaska-Aleutian Megathrust Fault released pressure that had slowly built up as the Pacific Plate slipped underneath the North American Plate. According to scientists, the fracture responsible for the temblor occurred 16 miles (25 km) underground.

Following the March 27, 1964 Great Alaskan Earthquake, fissures along Seward Highway near Anchorage, Alaska, made travel difficult.

Help from Celebrities

Dozens of international celebrities appeared in the Hope for Haiti Now telethon, which raised $58 million. A collection of musical performances from the telethon raced to number one on the iTunes chart, raising even more money for Haiti.

U.S. music producer Quincy Jones and singer-songwriter Lionel Richie organized more than eighty artists to record a new version of "We Are the World," a song written in 1985 to raise money for African famine relief.

British music producer Simon Cowell brought together another group of recording artists. They sang "Everybody Hurts" by R.E.M. for a documentary video that features video footage of disaster victims being helped. Thanks to help from people all over the world, Haiti has made great strides. But there is more work to be done and the struggle continues to keep people healthy and find them safe housing.

On January 22, 2010, pop artists Rihanna and Bono performed live in London as part of the Hope for Haiti Now telethon.

Help from Ordinary Citizens

Even more money came from individuals and local groups. In many countries, schools and community organizations held fund-raisers. In North America, kids raised money with lemonade stands, bake sales, and bike-a-thons.

Eight-year-old Madi Cummins, a second-grader at Berea Community School in Berea, Kentucky, displays the containers she decorated and distributed to the other elementary classrooms to collect money for the Haiti earthquake relief effort. The fund-raising program Madi participated in raised $1,300 for the American Red Cross.

Rescue workers search for victims and survivors after an apartment complex collapsed during an earthquake in Concepción, Chile, on February 27, 2010.

The Quakes Continue

The 9.5 magnitude quake that shook the west coast of south central Chile in 1960 relieved a lot of pressure along the boundary between the Nazca Plate and South American Plates. But it wasn't enough to prevent future temblors.

Just five years later, another major earthquake struck the coastal city of La Ligua. Quakes have continued to shake, rattle, and roll the region ever since. On March 3, 1985, and then ten years later on July 30, 1995, temblors with magnitudes of 8.0 caused significant damage in Chile.

On February 27, 2010, the third most powerful earthquake ever recorded in Chile struck the city of Concepción. It killed at least seven hundred people and damaged about 1.5 million homes. The 8.8-magnitude temblor was even more powerful than the quake that devastated Haiti just a month earlier.

Major Chilean Quakes, 1570–1949

Date	Location	Magnitude
1965	La Ligua	7.1
1971	Illapel	7.5
1985	Santiago	8.0
1987	Antofagasta	7.2
1995	Antofagasta	8.0
2005	Tarapacá	7.8
2007	Antofagasta	7.7
2010	Concepción	8.8

EARTHQUAKE ACTIVITY: CAN I GET A WITNESS?

Did an earthquake recently occur in your town? Chances are someone you know remembers at least a minor tremor. When you find a friend or neighbor who has experienced an earthquake, record an eyewitness account for future generations.

1. Ask the person to tell his or her story. You can write it down, record it on a voice recorder, or videotape it.

2. Ask lots of questions: Where was the person when the earthquake hit? What was he or she doing? How long did the shaking last? Was there any damage?

3. Get some information about the storyteller. You should include his or her full name, date of birth, address, and the interview date.

4. If possible, include photocopies or photographs or videotape the photos of any damage the earthquake caused.

5. Finished? Consider donating a copy of your eyewitness account to a local historical society. Future generations will want to know what happened first hand.

• •

Reelfoot Lake in Tennessee formed as a giant wave of water from the Mississippi River flowed backward and crashed down over the land during the February 7, 1812 earthquake.

New Madrid Earthquakes

Where: Mississippi River Valley, United States
When: December 16, 1811; January 23, 1812; February 7, 1812
Magnitude: 8.6, 8.4, 8.8

California's famous quakes aren't even the second most powerful temblors in North America. That honor goes to a series of three violent shake ups that occurred along the New Madrid Fault in 1811 and 1812.

The New Madrid Fault lies beneath Mississippi River, extending from Memphis, Tennessee, to Vienna, Illinois. Quakes along the fault have had epicenters in Illinois, Missouri, Kentucky, Arkansas, and Tennessee.

Hundreds of minor tremors shake the area each year, but the massive quakes 200 years ago caused the ground to roll in giant waves. In some places, the land cracked wide open. In other areas, the ground rose or sank, causing flooding that destroyed forests and formed new swamps and lakes. The course of the Mississippi River changed, and homes and fields were buried by landslides. People felt the shaking as far away as Boston, Massachusetts.

Only a few people died in the New Madrid earthquakes in 1811 and 1812 because the area was sparsely populated. But today, millions of people live in the areas most affected by the shaking.

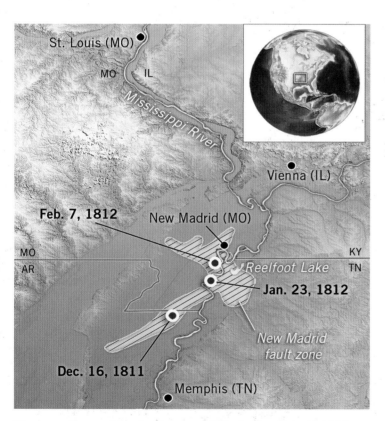

Three major earthquakes occurred along the New Madrid Fault in 1811 and 1812. And it could be the site of the next big U.S. earthquake. Scientists say there's a 90 percent chance of a magnitude 6.0 or greater quake striking the area before 2040.

I Was There!

The well-known naturalist and artist John James Audubon described the January 23, 1812 earthquake in his journal. "[A]ll the trees and shrubs began to move from their roots. The ground rose and fell in successive furrows like the ruffled waters of a lake."

Chile's Massive Quakes

Where: West coast of Chile
When: May 22, 1960
Magnitude: 9.5

Chile—a long, narrow country on the west coast of South America—has a lengthy history of powerful earthquakes. Just off Chile's west coast, the Nazca Plate is slowly sinking into the mantle as the South American Plate rides up over it. As time passes, the rock on either side of the fault reaches its breaking point. Then the crust cracks and shifts, and waves of destruction shake the surface.

In the 379 years between 1570 and 1949, towns along the Chilean coast have endured 11 major temblors. One of the most destructive quakes struck south central Chile on January 24, 1939. It killed 28,000 people and left 700,000 homeless.

Major Chilean Quakes, 1570–1949

Date	Location	Magnitude
1570	Concepción	8.3
1575	Valdivia	8.5
1647	Santiago	8.5
1751	Concepción	8.5
1835	Concepción	8.5
1868	Arica	9.0
1906	Valparaíso	8.2
1922	Vallenar	8.5
1939	Chillán	8.3
1943	Coquimbo	8.2
1949	Tierra del Fuego	7.8

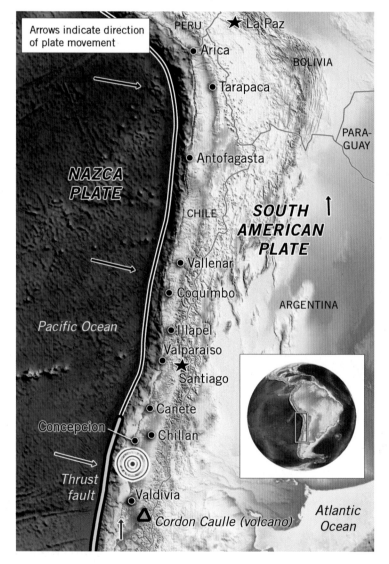

Chile has a long history of earthquakes. All of the cities and coastal towns shown on this map have experienced major temblors as the Nazca Plate moves below the thicker South American Plate.

In Anchorage, Alaska, dozens of streets were left cracked and torn as waves of destruction shook the city.

I Was There!

Eleven-year-old Georgiana Llaneza lived in Anchorage, Alaska, when the Prince William Sound earthquake struck. She remembers "The radio crashed to the floor, our dinner flew off the stove, chairs scooted and fell, . . . I lost my balance as my feet hit the wobbling tile. I tried to stand again, and fell after one or two steps. . . . I scrambled and ran, but as the earth continued to shake violently, I once again fell . . . Mother hurtled over me with the baby in her arms, screaming in a voice raw with fear and despair, 'Get Out! Get Out! Get Out!' As I watched her disappear through the front doorway, suddenly a fierce emotion seized me, and I began to crawl furiously on all fours. By the time I reached the front doorway, the earth's shaking had stopped."

The Great Chilean Quake

With such a devastating history of earthquakes, people in Chile have learned to take even minor shaking seriously. When residents in Valdivia and Puerto Montt felt tremors on the afternoon of May 22, 1960, they ran into the street. Luckily, many of them were still outdoors when the most powerful earthquake in recorded history struck about 30 minutes later.

Within Minutes

As you can see in this photo of Valdivia, the Chilean temblor caused tremendous damage. About 2,000 people were killed by collapsing buildings and more than 2 million people were left homeless.

Within an Hour

Landslides triggered by the earthquake blocked the San Pedro River, causing the level of Riñihue Lake to rise quickly. People worked furiously to build and reinforce dams that would prevent flooding, but the next day some water did flow through. Several villages and parts of Valdivia flooded.

Believe It or Not

All eleven of the major temblors that shook Chile between 1570 and 1949 were more powerful than any of the quakes California experienced during the twentieth century.

15 Hours Later

38 Hours Later

15 Hours Later

The earthquake also caused a massive tsunami that raced across the Pacific Ocean. About 15 hours later, eight massive waves crashed onto Hilo, Hawaii. They killed sixty-one people and destroyed $75 million of property. In this photo you can see that the force of the waves knocked over a telephone pole and bent a metal lamp post to the ground.

38 Hours Later

The Valdivia Earthquake caused the vulcano Cordón Caulle to blow its top on May 24. During its dramatic two-month eruption, the volcano belched tons of rocks, ash, and gases up to 5 miles (8 km) into the sky. Lava flowed down the volcano's slopes, destroying everything in its path.

PREDICTING AND PREPARING

Scientists at Work

Each year, our planet experiences about 140 earthquakes with magnitudes of 6.0 or greater. These temblors are powerful enough to cause at least some damage to homes, schools, and other buildings. The strongest of them can lead to hundreds or even thousands of deaths.

Because earthquakes can cause so much death and destruction, scientists are working hard to understand them better. The more we know about temblors, the better we will become at predicting and preparing for them.

Scientists use several kinds of instruments to monitor the rock around known faults. They use tiltmeters to keep an eye on the tilt, or slope, of the land. Even a slight change may be a sign that rocks are shifting and could break soon.

Scientists use seismographs to measure the vibrations spreading through Earth. If they notice many small earthquakes occurring in an area, they pay close attention. Small quakes are often a warning that rocks are unstable and a larger temblor is on its way.

Even with all this equipment, scientists still can't predict earthquakes consistently and reliably. Every earthquake is different. Because the forces that cause rocks to snap are at work deep below Earth's surface, it's hard to know exactly when a temblor will occur and how destructive it will be. Still, scientists keep trying because predicting earthquakes can save lives.

John Cassidy reads the seismograph chart at the Pacific Geoscience Center of the Pacific from the earthquake that shook Victoria, British Columbia, Canada, on February 28, 2001. The temblor has a magnitude of 6.8. Its epicenter was located southwest of Seattle, Washington.

On and On

Most earthquakes last less than 1 minute, but some temblors shake the earth for up to 10 minutes.

Tweet, Tweet

In 2009, the U.S. Geological Survey developed a quick and inexpensive way to learn about earthquakes as they're happening. By monitoring the flow of earthquake report tweets, written by people using the popular social network Twitter, scientists can easily discover how widely an earthquake is felt and how strongly it shakes various areas. Using this information, scientists can pinpoint the origin and magnitude of a quake almost instantly.

● ● ● ● ● ● ● ● ● ● ●

Scientists Michael Poland (left) and Dan Dzurisin (right) set up a Global Positioning System (GPS) station near the lava dome of Mount St. Helens in Washington state. More than a dozen GPS stations have been installed on or around Mount St. Helens to measure ground-surface deformations that signal earthquakes may occur soon.

Muddy Water and Nervous Animals

Because several plates come together in China, the country has many active faults and a long history of powerful earthquakes. In fact, three of the ten deadliest temblors ever recorded happened in China.

Like modern scientists, ancient Chinese scholars recognized that small quakes often come before a larger one. They also noted that horses, cattle, pigs, rats, cats, dogs, birds, snakes, and other animals often act strangely before a temblor. And they observed that the water level in wells may change just before an earthquake. Sometimes the water turns muddy.

For many years, scientists ignored these accounts from China and similar ones from Europe. However, growing evidence shows that they can be used to predict temblors—at least sometimes.

In 1975, Chinese scientists noticed many small quakes near Haicheng. The land was tilting and local people had reported that well water was muddy. Both pets and farm animals seemed upset. Chinese officials told people to evacuate. The next day, a major quake devastated the area. Experts say the evacuation saved more than 150,000 lives.

Eyewitness accounts of animals acting strangely before earthquakes come from all over the world and date back hundreds of years. They include observations of bears and snakes coming out of hibernation early, pigs biting one another, horses and cattle breaking out of their stalls, deer herding in open fields, cats moving kittens outdoors, dogs howling for hours, birds making strange calls, and more.

I Was There!

After experiencing an earthquake in Lima, Peru, the eighteenth-century French explorer De La Barbinais Le Gentil wrote that "half an hour before the earth moves, all animals are seized with terror; horses whinny, tear their halters, and flee from the stalls; dogs bark, birds are terrified; rats and mice come out of their holes . . ."

Warned by the Dragon

A Chinese man named Zhang Heng invented the world's first seismograph nearly 1,900 years ago. Heng's seismograph had a pendulum inside. When an earthquake shook the ground, the pendulum would swing. Its motion would cause one of the dragons on the outside of the seismograph to release a bronze ball held in its mouth. The ball would drop into the mouth of a toad and make a sound that let people know when and in which direction an earthquake had occurred.

A Real Record Setter

During the last three thousand years, earthquakes in China have killed more than thirteen million people. No country has experienced greater loss from temblors.

This replica of Zhang Heng's astonishing seismograph was built in 2005.

Planning Ahead

Scientists can't prevent earthquakes, and so far, they can't predict exactly when or where they'll strike. But when communities and their citizens plan ahead, people have a better chance of surviving a quake.

Town and city officials can make sure that schools, hospitals, and fire stations are built on stable land. Schools and businesses can have earthquake drills, so people learn that they should crouch under sturdy furniture or stand in a doorway.

Families can develop emergency action plans too. Find out how on page 45. You can also check with the U.S. Geological Survey, the American Red Cross, or the Federal Emergency Management Agency. These groups all have guidelines that families can follow.

Being prepared for emergencies is always a good idea. But you probably don't need to worry too much about earthquakes. Even though temblors are a fact of life, most of them cause little if any damage. Scientists all over the world are learning more about Earth's plates and faults all the time. They share the information with engineers, architects, and city planners, so that people living in earthquake zones have a better chance of staying safe when an earthquake does strike.

People in Japan take the threat of quakes seriously. In this photo, people living and working in Tokyo's Ginza district are participating in an earthquake drill. This kind of emergency preparedness planning helped save lives during the devastating 9.0-magnitude Tōhoku earthquake and tsunami that struck Japan in March 2011.

With the help of a computer-controlled shake table and steel building models, a scientist demonstrates that buildings vibrate at different frequencies. If the frequency of the ground motion during an earthquake is close to the building's natural frequency, the building will probably topple over.

EARTHQUAKE ACTIVITY: GET PREPARED!

When is the best time to figure out what to do during an earthquake? Now. Here's how to get ready:

1.
Have flashlights, a first aid kit, a battery-operated radio, and a fire extinguisher on hand.

2.
Prepare a three-day supply of bottled water and canned food. Don't forget a can opener too.

3.
Know where to go! Ask your parents to help you find the safest place in your home. Plan where family members will meet if you get separated.

4.
Remind your family that aftershocks can occur. Everyone should wear a helmet and sturdy shoes after a quake.

Engineers and Architects at Work

Ask a scientist, an engineer, and an architect about the dangers of earthquakes and they'll all say the same thing: "Earthquakes don't kill people. Buildings kill people." They're right!

Most of the people who die in earthquakes are crushed when buildings collapse. The best way to save lives is to design buildings that can take a good shaking and still stand tall. Buildings in danger zones should have flexible steel frames and deep, solid foundations. That way they can absorb and resist shaking. The buildings should be made of fire-resistant materials. All the furniture and heavy equipment inside should be bolted to floors or walls.

Today new buildings in cities such as San Francisco, Los Angeles, and Tokyo are constructed with earthquakes in mind. So far, it looks like the hard work of architects and engineers is paying off.

In 1988, an earthquake with a magnitude of 6.8 struck Spitak, Armenia. It destroyed the city and killed more than 25,000 people. A year later, an earthquake with a magnitude of 6.9 struck San Francisco, California. Fewer buildings were destroyed and only 63 people died. Safer building practices made all the difference.

The Transamerica Pyramid is San Francisco, California, was designed to be twice as strong as building codes require. Its shape and structure help to make it earthquake proof.

Shake It Up!

Where is the best place to be during a powerful quake? Maybe a straw hut.

Tests performed at the University of Nevada show that small homes made of stacked bales of straw wrapped in nylon netting and sandwiched between layers of plaster can stand up to shaking twice as powerful as the magnitude 6.6 Northridge Earthquake that struck Los Angeles, California, in 1994.

According to Darcey Donovan, the founder of Pakistan Straw Bale and Appropriate Building, the straw home is perfect for people living in developing countries because "it's [tough] enough to save their lives, but it's affordable."

Words to Know

aftershocks an earthquake that follows and is triggered by another earthquake

crust the outer layer of Earth

earthquake a series of vibrations that radiates through Earth's interior

epicenter the point on Earth's surface that is directly above the focus of an earthquake

faults cracks that form in areas of Earth's crust as rocks shift. Most fractures occur in places where two or more plates meet.

focus the place from which an earthquake radiates out

intensity a measure of the damage done by an earthquake

magnitude a measure of the amount of energy released by an earthquake or volcano

mantle the layer of Earth between the crust and outer core. It is made of soft rock called magma.

tectonic plates the large slabs of rock that make up Earth's crust

temblors another name for earthquakes

Find Out More

Websites to Visit

Earthquakes
http://www.fema.gov/kids/
quake.htm

Earthquakes for Kids
http://earthquake.usgs.gov/
learn/kids/

San Andreas Fault
http://pubs.usgs.gov/gip/
earthq3/intro.html

Understanding Earthquakes
http://www.crustal.ucsb.edu/
ics/understanding/

World-wide Earthquake Locator
http://tsunami.geo.ed.ac.uk/local-
bin/quakes/mapscript/home.pl

Books to Read

Downs, Sandra. *When the Earth Moves.* Brookfield, CT: Twenty-First Century Books, 2000.

Grace, Catherine O'Neill. *Forces of Nature.* Washington, D.C.: National Geographic, 2004.

Sutherland, Lin. *Earthquakes and Volcanoes.* New York: Reader's Digest, 2000.

Van Rose, Sandra. *Volcano & Earthquake.* New York: DK Publishing, 2004.

Bibliography

An, Vickie. "Haiti Picks Up the Pieces." *Time for Kids,* January 29, 2010, p. 4–5.

Battersby, Stephen. "House of Straw." *Current Science,* November 27, 2009, pp. 8–9.

Fradin, Judy, and Dennis Fradin. *Earthquake: Eyewitness to Disaster.* Washington, D.C.: National Geographic, 2007.

Fradkin, Philip L. *Magnitude 8: Earthquakes and Life along the San Andreas Fault.* New York: Henry Holt and Company, 1998.

Gallardo, Eduardo. "Powerful earthquake rattles northern Chile, killing at least eight people." *The America's Intelligence Wire.* June 14, 2005.

"The Great Alaska Earthquake of 1964." Alaska Earthquake Information Center. http://www.aeic.alaska.edu/quakes/Alaska_1964_earthquake.html (Accessed February 6, 2010).

"Historic Earthquakes." U.S. Geological Survey. http://earthquake.usgs.gov/earthquakes/states/events/1964_03_28.php (Accessed February 6, 2010).

Guzzetti, Brian M. "High and Dry." *Birder's World.* December 2008, pp. 22–27.

Hough, Susan Elizabeth. "The Aftershocks that Weren't." *Natural History,* March 2001, 65–69.

Jacobson, Sherry. "Scientists say man-made reservoirs, drilling can trigger earthquakes," *Dallas Morning News,* June 14, 2009, http://www.dallasnews.com/sharedcontent/dws/news/localnews/ stories/DN-drillingsidebar_14met.ART.State.Edition1.50ce6fe.html (Accessed January 25, 2010).

Kerr, Richard A. "Continuing Indonesian Quakes Putting Seismologists on the Edge." *Science.* September, 21 2007, p. 1661.

Kerr, Richard A. "Foreshadowing Haiti's Catastrophe." *Science.* January 22, 2010, p. 398.

Mott, Maryann. "Can Animals Sense Earthquakes?" *National Geographic News.* November 11, 2003. http://news.nationalgeographic.com/news/2003/11/1111_031111_earthquakeanimals.html (Accessed January 29, 2010).

Perkins, Sid. "Seismology in Your Twitter Feed." *Science News,* January 16, 2010, p. 15.

"The Simon Cowell All-Stars Sing For Haiti." *All Things Considered,* February 2, 2010, 20:00–21:00 p.m.

Stewart, David, and Ray Knox. *The Earthquake America Forgot.* Marble Hill, MO: Guten-Richter Publications, 1995.

Tributsch, Helmut. *When the Snakes Awake: Animals and Earthquake Prediction.* Cambridge, MA: The MIT Press, 1982.

"We Are the World: 25 for Haiti Charity Single." *BBC News.* February 2, 2010. http://news.bbc.co.uk/2/hi/entertainment/8493915.stm (Accessed February 10, 2010).

Source Notes

Page 14: "Did you ever . . . almost as dreadful." Personal letter from Warren Olney of Oakland, California, to A. J. Ralston in Louisville, Kentucky, May 3, 1906, http://content.cdlib.org/view?docId=hb9j49p3qv&brand=calisphere&doc.view=entire_text (Accessed January 26, 2010).

Page 21: "the most likely place on the planet." Kerr, Richard A. "Continuing Indonesian Quakes Putting Seismologists on the Edge." *Science.* September, 21 2007, p. 1661.

Page 29: "[W]e heard a . . . on the street." From a January 14, 2010 post on the "Adventures in Life" blog. http://kimandpatrick.blogspot.com/search?updated-max=2010-01-20T17%3A08%3A00-08%3A00&max-results=10 (Accessed February 8, 2010).

Page 31: "The radio crashed . . . shaking had stopped." As told to Tom Irvine, Shock, Vibration & Acoustics Engineer at Dynamic Concepts Inc., Huntsville, Alabama, http://www.vibrationdata.com/earthquakes/alaska.htm (Accessed February 8, 2010)

Page 32: "all the trees . . . of a lake." Stewart, David and Ray Knox. *The Earthquake America Forgot.* (Guten-Richter Publications, 1995) p. 183.

Page 40: "half an hour . . . of their holes . . ." from Le Gentil's *Voyage Around the World* (1716) as quoted in Tributsch, Helmut (translated by Paul Langner). *When Snakes Awake: Animals and Earthquake Prediction* (MIT Press, 1982), p. 14.

Page 43: "it's enough to . . . but it's affordable." Battersby, Stephen. "House of Straw." *Current Science,* November 27, 2009, p. 8.

Index